**learning
and skills
development
agency**

making quality sense
a guide to quality, tools
and techniques, awards and
the thinking behind them

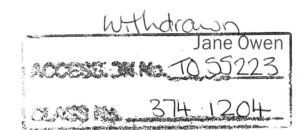

Published by the Learning and Skills Development Agency

www.LSDA.org.uk

Feedback should be sent to:
Information Services
Learning and Skills Development Agency
Regent Arcade House
19–25 Argyll Street
London W1F 7LS.
Tel 020 7297 9144
Fax 020 7297 9242
enquiries@LSDA.org.uk

Registered with the Charity Commissioners

Copyeditor: Karin Fancett
Designers: Dave Shaw and Tania Field
Cover illustration: Joel Quartey
Printer: Blackmore Ltd, Shaftesbury, Dorset

ISBN 1 85338 760 6

© Learning and Skills Development Agency 2002

1201A/07/02/4000

Further information

For further information about the issues discussed
in this publication please contact:
Jane Owen
Development Adviser
Learning and Skills Development Agency.
Tel 020 7297 9083
jowen@LSDA.org.uk

**This publication was funded by the Learning and Skills Council
as part of a contracted support and development programme.**

Contents

Introduction

Quality management is now a part of all sectors and its language has become part of everyday business speech. However, the terminology can be off-putting for people who are not part of the quality profession, and quality and the different gurus and theories can seem confusing. Books on quality are often fairly heavy tomes, and as a result the world of quality management can remain closed to many people.

The truth is that quality is based on common-sense principles that most people can easily understand. The practices and theories are as applicable to education and training as they are to any other sector. This publication is intended to guide you through some of the commonly used tools, techniques and theories. It is not comprehensive but will, I hope, give you a basic knowledge of the subject and point you towards further reading and organisations should you need to find out more.

The basics

Quality

There are many definitions of quality, including:

- conforming to requirements
- fitness for purpose
- meeting customer needs
- exceeding customer needs.

The common link between all of these definitions is the customer. Conforming to requirements and fitness for purpose, even if they are the requirements and purpose of the organisation, should be based on delivering quality products and services to the customer. All organisations, even those who believe their prime objective is making profit, survive by delivering customer needs.

Remember that meeting customer needs is not the same as meeting customer wants. For example, the service or product customers want might be so costly that they could not afford to pay for it. In such a case it would not meet their needs. There is no point in offering a Rolls-Royce to someone who can only afford a family saloon.

There are a number of quality methods that are used in organisations, the following are the the most common.

Quality control (QC) This is a method of controlling the quality of goods or services by having a system in place that monitors the quality of goods throughout the production process. A reliable quality control system will prevent goods or services that do not meet the required standard either reaching the end of the production process or being given to customers. If errors are found they are corrected.

Quality assurance (QA) This is a method of both assuring the quality of the final goods or services, as well as assuring the quality of processes. It requires planned and documented systems and processes that identify failures in design, production or delivery of goods or services before they become problems. It also requires those systems and processes to be audited and reviewed to ensure their ongoing suitability.

Total quality management (TQM) This involves integrating quality systems into every aspect of an organisation's operation. It is a management model that is based on the philosophy that quality is the responsibility of everyone in an organisation and that all systems within the organisation should support that philosophy. It requires a management-led commitment to continuous improvement and recognises that the customer is central to an organisation.

With all of these techniques it must be remembered that though inspection will identify errors, quality cannot be improved by inspection alone.

Processes

Processes are the building blocks of every organisation. It is important that each organisation understands its processes, how they work, what internal and external influences there are on them, their inputs and outputs.

Processes are often confused with documented procedures and can be seen as bureaucratic additions to already paper-laden work. The related documentation that many object to can hide the fact that everything we do, in work or out of it, is a process.

One technical definition of a process is an activity or a series of activities that changes an input into an output. In the learning and skills sector, inputs can include requests for information, letters of complaint or books. Outputs can include qualifications, learning or data.

Simply put, a process is something we do to add value to a product, an idea or a service. In its simplest form it can be illustrated as shown in Figure 1.

Figure 1 Diagrammatic representation of a process

Process knowledge and process management is key to any organisation-wide quality system.

More information on process management and improvement is given in the following chapter.

Customers

Customer is a term that has been increasingly used and abused in all sectors over the past years. It is easy to get hung up on the terminology of customer service instead of looking at service improvement. Most of us have experienced being called a customer while clearly not being treated as one. For example, announcements that tell overheated, delayed train passengers to make room for other customers do not make them feel like valued customers. In fact, such announcements can make them feel annoyed or patronised, especially when the service or the attitude of staff does not match the words.

There is emerging evidence that overusing the term customer can alienate the very people you are trying to serve. A recent NHS survey, for example, showed that people being treated wanted to be called patients. It is not what term is used by an organisation that is important, it is the way people are treated.

Customers are simply people to whom we give a service, be they learners, employers or funders and regardless of whether they pay directly or indirectly for the service. Each group will have its own needs and expectations and the service we provide to them has to reflect this. It is our responsibility to ensure that the service is provided for each group and individual to a quality that would satisfy us if we were the customer.

Internal customers

We all have customers though not everyone deals with external customers. A good indicator of how well an organisation will treat its external customers is how well its staff treat their internal customers.

Internal customers are your colleagues. They are anyone to whom you provide a service. It is important to ensure that they are satisfied with the service you provide for them.

Customer complaints

A complaint could be described as any expression of dissatisfaction from a customer. Generally, if a customer believes he or she is making a complaint then it is a complaint.

For every person who makes a complaint around 20 will say nothing to you but will either stop using your service or will stay unsatisfied with you. So, if they have gone to the trouble of making a complaint they usually feel genuinely disgruntled.

Again, it is important that we do not become tied up in the technicality of language. Some organisations can over-complicate their complaints procedure by stratifying complaints using categories such as minor, formal, informal, verbal, written, major, etc.

This does not mean that complaints should not be coded to assist analysis. Coding is an important means of identifying root causes of problems, but it is not something that customers need to know about.

How an organisation recovers from service failure is one of the most important aspects of its service delivery. Research has shown that customers who complain and have their problems resolved quickly are more likely to repeat purchase than customers who had no problems with the service or organisation.

Though it is best to get things right first time, a well-handled complaint can leave customers more satisfied with an organisation than if the service had not failed at all.

There are times when you cannot do what your customer wants you to do. If this happens you should always be willing and able to explain why you cannot do it. There is nothing more likely to infuriate a customer who is making a complaint than a 'job's worth' attitude.

Responses such as 'it's not our policy' or 'it's not my job' are more likely to antagonise the situation than explaining why something cannot be done and making a useful suggestion about an alternative service or action.

There are some basic principles that are common to organisations that make good use of customer complaint feedback.

Access and information How easy is it for your customers to tell you when something goes wrong ? An organisation that boasts of very low complaint rates may in fact just be inaccessible. Make it easy for your customer to let you know that something has gone wrong and consider how your customers prefer to communicate with you.

Staff knowledge and access Publicity about the complaints procedure should not be confined to customers. Some organisations give each staff member a full copy of the complaints procedure or make it available on the organisation's intranet. Alternatively, some organisations produce leaflets for staff that explain the reasons why complaints procedures are needed and what the processes are that should be followed.

Reporting Both what is reported and who it is reported to send out strong messages about the importance given to successful complaint handling.

Organisations should beware of using the number of complaints received as a performance indicator. If staff feel they will be penalised for reporting complaints made about themselves or their services it becomes easier simply not to report them. Remember a low number of logged complaints is as likely to be caused by the inaccessibility of the complaints process as by high satisfaction levels.

Some alternative performance indicators are :

- time taken to make initial response to complaints
- time taken to resolve complaints
- complaint type
- number of improvements made as a result of complaints
- number of complaints that are passed on to the review panel
- satisfaction with complaint response.

Reporting on complaints should be part of the management cycle. Senior management should be aware of the nature and causes of complaints and the resource implications of putting corrective actions and resultant improvements in place.

Benchmarking

Benchmarking, at its simplest, is a way of comparing something, whether it is a product, service, process or output, to establish the relative level of performance.

There are three distinct types of benchmarking.

Metric benchmarking This involves the comparison of statistical data. Usually the data compared is a performance indicator, for example customer satisfaction levels, costs or staff turnover. The results are often compiled in a league table. It is a relatively low-cost method. It shows how an organisation's results compare with other organisations but does not explain why there is a difference.

Diagnostic benchmarking This involves examining how an organisation operates and comparing this with how other organisations operate. It is a method of identifying what processes might be causing particularly good or poor results. It helps to identify areas of comparative strength and weakness within an organisation and pinpoints where to focus effort when making improvements.

Process benchmarking This is a systematic method of comparing specific processes with other processes within the organisation or within other organisations. It is quite resource intensive but has the potential to give impressive results. It is explained in more detail in the following chapter.

A comparison of the efforts / resources / costs and knowledge / benefits of these three types of benchmarking is shown in Figure 2.

Figure 2 Relationship between effort and results for different types of benchmarking

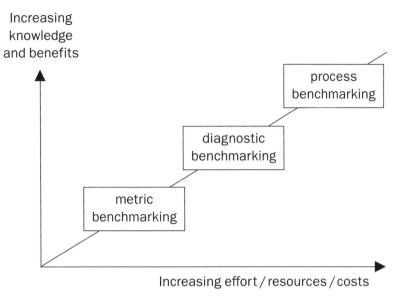

Processes, processes, processes

Processes are the building blocks of an organisation and so their management, review and improvement are fundamental to its success.

Before attempting to improve or manage processes it is important to understand them fully. In many organisations processes are documented in written procedures and quality manuals. These can form an excellent record of how the organisation operates and a useful reference for staff who need to know how things work.

Organisations that have not documented their processes should consider doing so as a matter of urgency. Rather than trying to produce text-based documents from scratch, organisations should start with flowcharts.

Producing flowcharts (see the chapter on tools and techniques) has a number of advantages. Apart from the obvious one of documenting what is done, a flowchart allows the staff producing it to take a fresh view of the process using a systematic approach. It is surprising how many potential improvements can be identified by producing a flowchart. Staff can also start to see how their work impacts on other people.

As well as identifying and documenting how the process works, it is important to establish the following.

The process owner Who is the person with overall responsibility for the process? (This is usually the manager.)

The process supplier Who or what does the process rely on to operate and how does the organisation feed back the process needs to the supplier?

The process customer Who or what does the process supply? How does the organisation ensure that the process customer is satisfied with the output of the process?

Once the details of a process are confirmed, work should begin on establishing how well it operates. The following questions might be asked.

- Does the process produce a product or service that meets customer requirements?
- Are there failures in the process operation?
- What is the cost of the process in terms of time, materials, equipment and overheads?
- How responsive is the process to the customer?

Continuous process improvement

Many people have difficulty with the concept of continuous improvement. They argue that if something is 'perfect' it cannot be improved. Processes may well produce exactly what they were designed to produce but it is unlikely that simply doing the same thing will result in a product or service that continues to meet customer needs.

Customers' needs change over time. Both internal and external customers tend to expect higher standards and shorter timescales, often at lower prices. Learners' expectations rise and funding and inspection bodies expect standards to rise. Costs change, technology changes and regulations change. The only way to ensure that a process continues to meet needs is to review it regularly.

Continuous process improvement is a systematic method of analysing data, identifying root causes of problems, understanding likely future changes to product or service requirements, and acting on the results. It involves ensuring that feedback from internal and external customers and staff is actually fed back to the right people and that the information is used to review and improve the process. Problems with the process are then identified and solutions are developed using a variety of quality tools (see the following chapter). Front-line staff tend to be heavily involved in this way of working, but need the support of senior management.

This constant review will help to ensure that the process, and hence the product or service it produces, continues to meet customer needs over time.

The key steps of continuous improvement are:

- document the process
- establish process suppliers / customers / owner
- measure the process
- identify problems
- identify solutions / improvements
- implement changes
- review changes
- start again.

Process re-engineering

Process re-engineering is a technique employed to make major step changes in quality. In many cases a re-engineering project starts (in theory) from the concept of 'the blank sheet of paper' or 'thinking the unthinkable'. In practice, it is rare that there will be a genuine start from scratch as the costs involved would be prohibitive.

Unlike continuous improvement, there is more of a top-down feel to process re-engineering. This does not mean that staff are not involved at all. They will eventually have to implement the new process and so it is usually beneficial to involve them to some extent.

The main steps of re-engineering are:

- decide on the scope of the project
- assemble a team
- gather data on the customer needs
- design a new process
- test the new process
- implement the new process.

Such re-engineering can result in substantial leaps in process quality, but if not dealt with properly can cause major problems. The main barriers to success when using this are:

- lack of long-term management commitment
- resistance to change
- unrealistic expectations
- cost implications.

Some of these barriers can be overcome by using a more incremental approach to the project.

Continuous process improvement versus process re-engineering

Table 1 compares continuous process improvement with process re-engineering.

Table 1 Comparing continuous improvement to re-engineering

	Continuous improvement	**Re-engineering**
Involvement	All staff	Project group
Type of change	Gradual, incremental	Sudden, major
Time-scale	Ongoing	Sudden, one-off
Personnel focus	Bottom-up with management support	Top-down with some staff input

Process benchmarking

Process benchmarking is a systematic method of improvement that uses others' good practice and learning to improve your own processes. It is a method of identifying what must be improved in an organisation, finding ways of making those improvements, and then implementing the improvements.

It requires an organisation to fully understand its processes and its customers' and stakeholders' needs. From that point it is possible to identify gaps between needs and performance.

Once an organisation knows what to improve it can use the knowledge and experience of the organisations it is benchmarking with – its benchmarking partners – to identify better ways of working.

Process benchmarking can be:

- **internal** learning from other departments within your organisation
- **sector specific** learning from organisations that are in a similar area of work
- **generic** learning from organisations that may operate in a totally different area.

There are four vital requirements that must be in place before starting a benchmarking project.

- Strong commitment from senior management to act on the findings of the project. Identify a suitable champion at senior level.
- Support for the staff taking part in the project, including training and resources. Training in quality tools is particularly useful.
- Authorisation for staff to develop, pilot and implement new practices where appropriate.
- Agreed time off from their normal duties for those staff taking part and arrangements in place to cover staff when they are working on the project.

Any process can be benchmarked. However, one of the most common reasons for failure in a benchmarking project is that the subject area was too wide and nebulous. Once people realise the benefits of benchmarking it is easy to become enthusiastic and to over-stretch. A common area identified for benchmarking is 'communication'. This issue, seemingly raised by every staff survey ever conducted, is so large that few organisations really understand how it works. As a result, any attempts to improve it, especially as a first project, through benchmarking tend to be problematic.

Before deciding to benchmark sizeable chunks of processes, it is necessary to consider the resources available, the experience of staff involved, the size of the problem (if known) and the importance of the process.

Process benchmarking steps

The following is a summary of the steps to be followed when conducting process benchmarking.

Identify and scope the process Be realistic about what can be tackled and the resources available.

Establish a benchmarking team Use staff who are involved in the process and who are customers or suppliers of the process. Do not rely solely on managers.

Ensure staff are trained Can they use the relevant quality tools? Do they understand the benchmarking process? Do not lose valuable staff input by not offering suitable training.

Document the process Use flowcharting to get a thorough picture of how the process operates. Be honest, and document how the process actually operates not how it might or should operate.

Establish the customer needs What outputs are required from the process? What inputs are required?

Identify gaps and duplications What does not work well? Where do problems occur? Is there any obviously unnecessary work?

Produce a benchmarking questionnaire What information is needed from a partner organisation? What documentation is available?

Identify benchmarking partners Internal or external? Specific or generic? Who is best at what you are looking at?

Contact potential partners Include details of the project, your process flowchart, the benchmarking questionnaire and a copy of the benchmarking code of conduct (see the Appendix) in your correspondence.

Conduct the visit to the partner Offer a reciprocal visit. Keep the partner informed of what has happened as a result of the visit.

Review the information gained Use the team to identify good practice found during the visit. Is any additional information required?

Implement changes Adapt good practice then adopt new methods. Do not assume that the partner organisation's methods will be a perfect fit for your organisation.

Review Has it worked? Are there more changes to be made?

Quality tools and techniques

The tools and techniques listed in this chapter are used to identify problems and to identify and implement solutions within an organisation or a department:

- affinity diagrams
- brainstorming
- cause and effect
- check sheets / tally sheets
- flowcharts
- force field analysis
- Gantt charts
- histograms
- moments of truth
- Pareto analysis
- scatter diagrams
- SWOT analysis.

They can be used with minimal training by staff at all levels and help to provide a more focused examination of quality issues.

Affinity diagrams

Affinity diagrams (Figure 3) are a way of sorting a variety of ideas, problems or issues into related groups or under specific headings. Affinity diagrams are usually constructed by a team of people.

Steps in constructing affinity diagrams

- The team identifies the possible issues, problems or ideas
  (try using brainstorming).
- Each issue, problem or idea identified is recorded on
  a separate card or Post-it note.
- The cards or notes are laid out randomly.
- The team begins to group each of the cards or notes, moving those
  that they do not agree with until everyone is happy with the grouping.
- A short description is produced for each grouping.
- The team identifies how the headings relate to each other.

Figure 3 An example of an affinity diagram

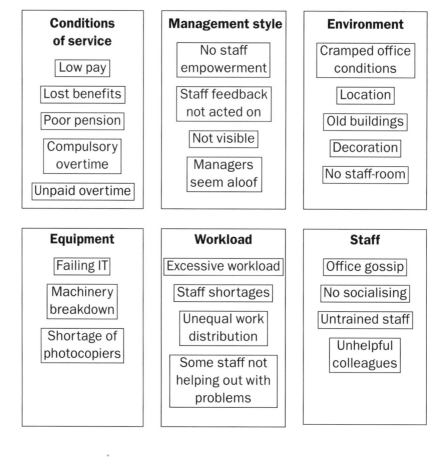

Staff morale problems

Brainstorming

Brainstorming is a simple way to generate a large number of ideas from a group of people in a relatively short period of time. The idea is that a group of people bounce ideas off each other. Even really impractical ideas are seen as useful as they can generate new ideas that are more practical.

Steps in brainstorming

- Write the problem on a board or flipchart.
- Choose a group leader.
- Assemble the group around the board or chart.
- Members of the team call out ideas for solving the problem. This can either be done in rotation or people can call out as they get ideas.
- All ideas are written up.
- Once the ideas are generated the team eliminates those that are unlikely to work and prioritises those that remain.

Brainstorming rules

- Everyone's comments and ideas are equally valid.
- All ideas must be recorded, no matter how off the wall they seem.
- There should be no criticism of ideas during the idea-generating part of the brainstorming.
- Think the unthinkable.

Cause and effect

The cause and effect diagram (Figure 4), sometimes called an Ishikawa diagram, is a graphical representation of the likely causes of problems in a process. Because of the shape of the diagram it is also sometimes referred to as fish bone analysis.

Figure 4 An example of a cause and effect diagram

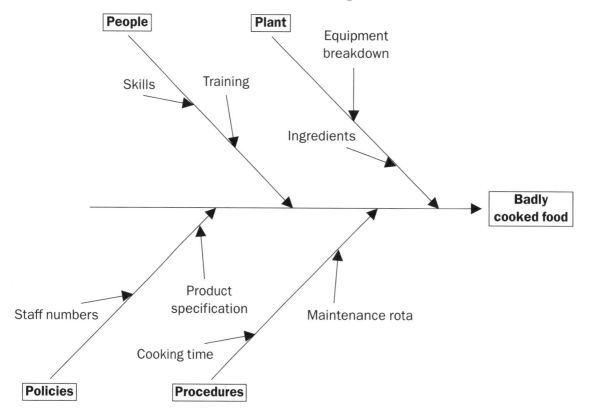

Each of the possible causes of a problem is drawn against a branch. One method used is the '5M' method, where each branch is assigned one of the following headings:

- machinery
- manpower
- method
- material
- maintenance.

In non-manufacturing organisations the '4P' method (see Figure 4) is often used:

- people
- plant (the equipment used)
- policies
- procedures.

Of course, each situation is different and it may be better to use your own headings.

The contributory causes of each of these main causes are then identified, usually using brainstorming.

The diagram is generally drawn up by a group of people who are involved in the process being examined. As with brainstorming, the method is guided by a facilitator who ensures that everyone can contribute to the discussion.

Check sheets / tally sheets

Check sheets / tally sheets (Figure 5) are simple methods of recording and displaying data. They need to be prepared in advance and can then be completed with ease.

Figure 5 An example of a check / tally sheet showing issues highlighted on a staff satisfaction survey for a college department

Date: 3 December 2001

Issue raised	Most important issue raised	Other issue raised
Management	|||	̶|̶|̶|̶|̶ ||
Staff morale / Appreciation			̶|̶|̶|̶|̶	
IT	||	
Salary	̶|̶|̶|̶|̶			
Workload	|||	|||
Other	||	̶|̶|̶|̶|̶ ||

Flowcharts

Flowcharts are diagrammatic representations of processes. They can be constructed using a very small number of symbols (Figure 6).

Figure 6 Flowchart symbols

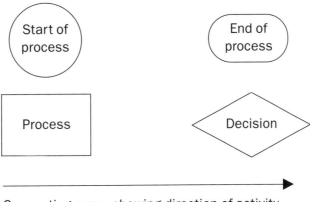

Connecting arrow showing direction of activity

There are many other symbols, but it is often best to keep to as small a number as practicable to ensure that as many people as possible can understand them.

Flowcharting is a way to make sure that you understand each stage in a process and how each stage links to the next stage. A flowchart is simply a pictorial description of a process that shows activities and their results in the order they take place (Figure 7). Though producing flowcharts is time consuming there are a number of benefits to using them. The interaction between activities becomes much clearer using a flowchart than looking at a text-based description. It is much easier to identify duplication of effort, and work that does not add to the value of the process.

Figure 7 An example of a flowchart

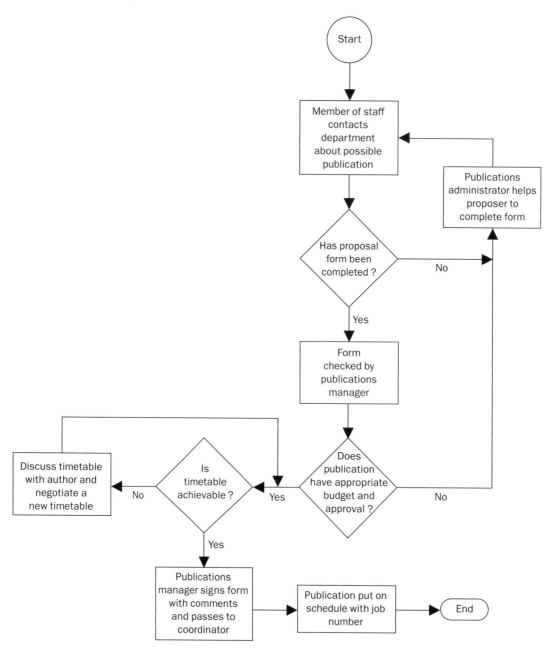

The following guidelines should be considered before flowcharting.

- The people who should develop the flowchart are those people involved in the process area.

- Use a facilitator who is not involved in the process to ask the obvious questions that people involved in the process are often not free to ask – 'why do this?', 'who is responsible?' and 'what is this for?'.

- Decide how detailed the flowchart will be before starting – it is easy to become so involved in the detail that the flowchart becomes unmanageable.

- The flowchart should initially be constructed using a wipe board or Post-it notes, as there will inevitably be a number of additions and changes to the chart as it is developed.

- Remember to flowchart what actually happens, not what should happen.

- Flowcharts often take longer to construct than anticipated. Allow for a second meeting where staff can bring along additional information highlighted during the first meeting.

Force field analysis

Force field analysis is a way of illustrating the positive and negative forces acting on a process. It allows an organisation to see what positive aspects need to be reinforced and what negative forces need to be dealt with.

A straight line, representing the process being analysed, is drawn down the centre of a sheet. Drivers and barriers are then added, drawn as arrows pointing away from the line. Positive forces (drivers) point in one direction and negative forces (barriers) point in the other.

To give additional detail the arrows can be 'weighted' – that is, drawn in proportion to their influence on the process.

Figure 8 shows some of the most probable positive and negative forces for a process of changing work methods at one organisation. The drivers and barriers would be different in each organisation and the length of the arrows would also depend on the culture and situation of the organisation.

Figure 8 An example of a force field diagram

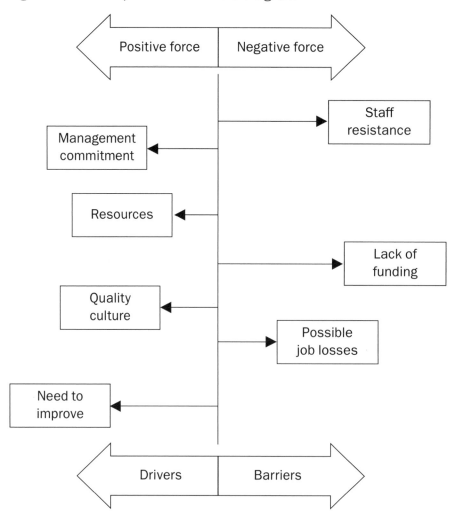

Gantt charts

A Gantt chart (Figure 9) is a useful method of planning and monitoring a project. It shows the progress of each element of a project on a separate line, plotted against the estimated or actual time for each element. The elements can run consecutively, or in parallel. Gantt charts show the likely overall timescale for projects and, by updating them regularly, it is possible to highlight any potential problems that could alter the completion date.

Though there are specific software packages available for constructing Gantt charts, they can be drawn by hand or by using a basic spreadsheet package.

Constructing a Gantt chart

- Split the project into 'bite-sized' elements.
- Estimate the time it will take to complete each element.
- Determine whether each element is dependent on the completion of a previous element before it can be started or completed.
- List the elements down one side of the sheet in time order of them starting.
- List the overall timescale along the top of the sheet.
- Draw in a block on each line showing the timescale for each element.

The chart should be updated regularly, using different colours or shading to show completed, current and pending elements of the project and altering timescales where appropriate.

Figure 9 An example of a Gantt chart

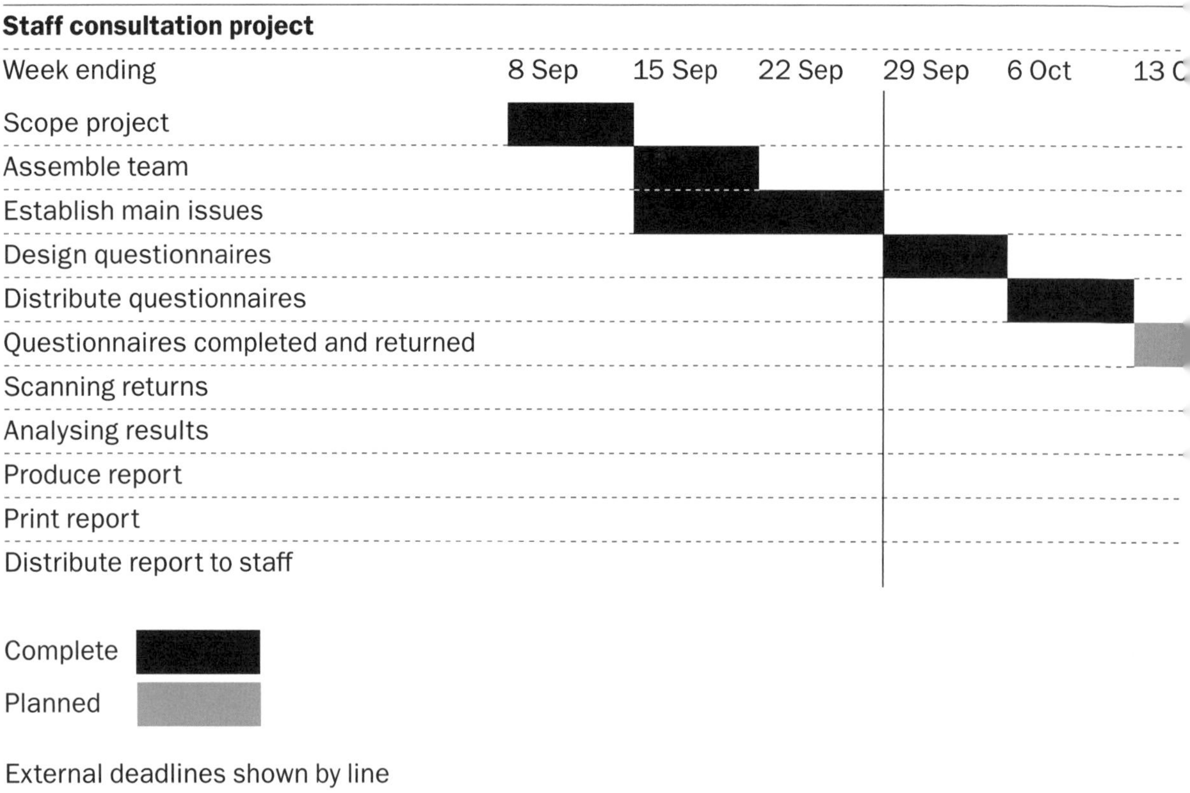

Staff consultation project

Week ending	8 Sep	15 Sep	22 Sep	29 Sep	6 Oct	13 O
Scope project						
Assemble team						
Establish main issues						
Design questionnaires						
Distribute questionnaires						
Questionnaires completed and returned						
Scanning returns						
Analysing results						
Produce report						
Print report						
Distribute report to staff						

Complete ▉

Planned ▉

External deadlines shown by line

0 Oct	27 Oct	3 Nov	10 Nov	17 Nov	24 Nov	1 Dec	8 Dec	15 Dec	22 Dec

Histograms

A histogram (Figure 10) is a bar chart that is used to demonstrate the variation in a set of data. It shows the frequency with which particular values occur and is a good method of illustrating the 'shape' of the distribution.

Figure 10 An example of a histogram

Learners on a course

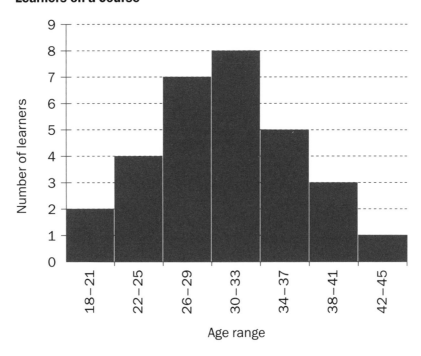

Moments of truth

Moments of truth (MoT) are the times when a customer comes into contact with a member of staff.

Organisations are often not aware of how many of these moments of truth there are. There is a tendency to concentrate on more obvious examples such as when a customer is greeted at reception or when a call is made to the service department. This can lead to less obvious moments of truth, such as when a customer makes a telephone call to the finance department or asks a cleaner for directions in a corridor, being ignored. It is often these less obvious moments of truth that are the 'make or break points' for customers when they are deciding whether they are satisfied.

It is a good idea for organisations to map moments of truth to establish what areas and processes they should review and what staff may need additional training.

Pareto analysis

Pareto was an Italian economist who realised that 85% of the country's wealth was in the hands of 15% of the people. This basic principle, sometimes called the 80/20 rule, appeared to be applicable to vast numbers of numerical facts.

Using this theory, we can assume that 80% of problems result from 20% of causes. In factories, for example, 80% of the value of the stock in storerooms is likely to be held by 20% of the items in stock. In surgeries, 80% of visits to GPs are likely to be made by 20% of registered patients.

A simple way to use this tool is to analyse the root cause of complaints and comments made over the past year. These root causes could then be categorised into groups and ranked according to how much they cost, how often they occur or how much time is spent solving the problems. By using the Pareto method to analyse the root cause of complaints you can focus on processes whose improvement will make the biggest difference to service delivery.

It is usual to portray the results as a Pareto diagram (Figure 11), a type of bar chart with the most frequently occurring or most costly area to the left of the diagram and the least to the right.

Figure 11 An example of a Pareto diagram

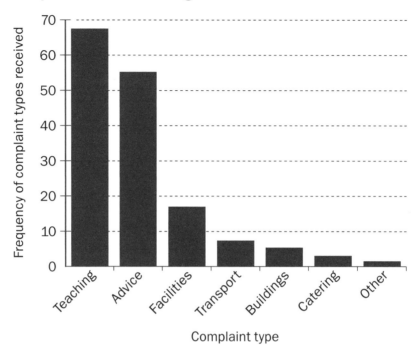

Complaints received in college X

Scatter diagrams

A scatter diagram is a chart that shows data by displaying the relationship between two variables. It is a way of finding out whether one variable (eg the number of hours a learner revises for an exam) is affected by another variable (eg the exam results) and whether the effect is positive or negative.

Figure 12 An example of a scatter diagram with positive correlation

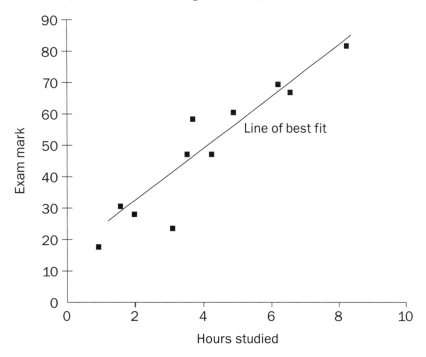

Figure 12 shows that for this mocked-up group of learners, the more they studied the better their exam results. This suggests that studying had a positive effect on exam results.

Other diagrams (Figure 13) might show a negative correlation.

Figure 13 An example of a scatter diagram with negative correlation

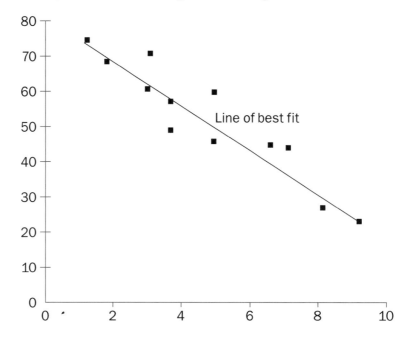

Line of best fit

The closer the data points are grouped around a theoretical straight line the stronger the relationship. Figures 14 and 15 show scatter diagrams with strong and weak relationships, respectively.

Figure 14 An example of a scatter diagram with a strong relationship

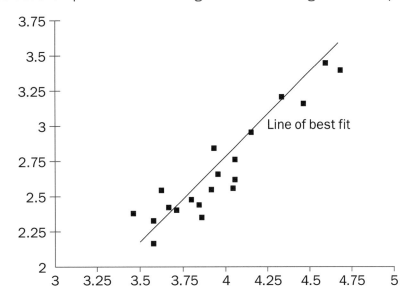

Figure 15 An example of a scatter diagram with a weak relationship

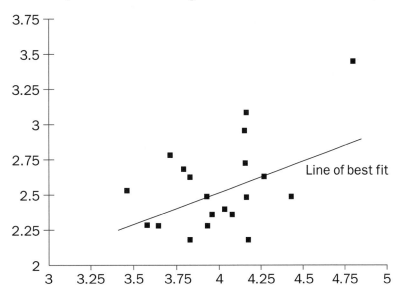

SWOT analysis

SWOT (strengths, weaknesses, opportunities, threats) analysis is a useful tool for establishing the strengths and weaknesses of a process, innovation, department or organisation.

The relevant issues are recorded against each of the four headings.

Example issues for strengths:

- what do we do well?
- what advantages do we have? (staff knowledge, good resources, good reputation, etc).

Example issues for weaknesses:

- what do we do badly?
- what needs improvement?
- what disadvantages do we have? (inadequate funding, staff shortages, poor reputation, etc).

Example issues for opportunities:

- social changes
- new technology
- government policy changes
- new funding
- additional customers.

Example issues for threats:

- competition
- declining customer base
- funding cuts
- high staff turnover.

It is always a good idea to involve others when going through this process, as one person is unlikely to be able to understand or recognise all of the issues. Use brainstorming to gather a more comprehensive view.

Models, awards and assessment

There are several quality models that are used by organisations in all sectors. Some models are intended to be a basis for self-assessment, others are used to demonstrate that organisations have reached specified quality standards and are externally assessed. Though each model has a slightly different focus they are all based on providing products and services that systematically meet customer needs and, through formalised reviews, ensure that the organisation concerned continues to meet those needs.

The five examples discussed in this chapter are:

- Charter Mark
- EFQM Excellence Model
- Investors in People
- ISO 9000
- PROBE (Promoting Business Excellence).

Charter Mark

The Charter Mark scheme is a customer service standard and an award promoted by the government. All public sector organisations that deal directly or indirectly with the public can apply to be awarded a Charter Mark.

Charter Marks are given to organisations by a panel of independent judges on the basis of the recommendations of a team of assessors.

To gain a Charter Mark an organisation has to fulfil the following ten criteria.

1 Set standards
2 Be open and provide full information
3 Consult and involve
4 Encourage access and the promotion of choice
5 Treat all fairly
6 Put things right when they go wrong
7 Use resources effectively
8 Innovate and improve
9 Work with other providers
10 Provide user satisfaction.

Applicants must send a 13-page written application explaining how they meet the criteria, along with supporting documentary evidence. The organisation is then visited by an assessor who gives detailed feedback on the visit and on the evidence provided. If the organisation is judged to have reached the required standard it is awarded a Charter Mark. Organisations wishing to retain their Charter Mark must be re-assessed every 3 years.

EFQM Excellence Model

The European Foundation for Quality Management (EFQM) Excellence Model is promoted in the UK by the British Quality Foundation (BQF). The model (Figure 16) is based on nine criteria; five of these are 'enablers' covering what an organisation does – leadership, people, policy and strategy, partnership and resources, and process – and four are 'results' covering what an organisation achieves – people results, customer results, society results and key performance results.

Figure 16 Diagram illustrating the EFQM Excellence Model

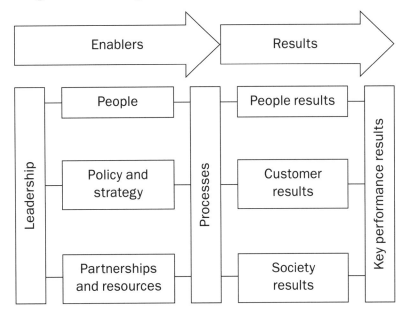

The model is designed to be used as a self-assessment tool, but if an organisation feels its performance against the model is of a sufficient level an external assessment can be requested to obtain a Quality Award. To apply for the award an organisation must submit a document for assessment. If shortlisted, the organisation is then visited and a jury considers the results of the visit.

The Excellence Model helps identify strengths and weaknesses, provides a benchmark against which an organisation can measure itself from year to year, and allows an organisation to compare itself against other organisations.

Investors in People

Investors in People (IiP) is an award that is given to organisations that meet criteria laid down for the training and development of people. It was developed in 1990 by the National Training Task Force, in collaboration with a number of well-respected organisations including the CBI (Confederation of British Industry), Trades Union Congress (TUC) and Institute of Personnel and Development (IPD).

It is based on the premise that an organisation cannot continue to be successful if it does not ally its people's skills with its business needs. Table 2 sets out the principles and indicators of the standards.

Table 2 Principles and indicators of IiP standards

© Investors in People UK 2000

Principles	Indicators
Commitment An Investor in People is fully committed to developing its people in order to achieve its aims and objectives	The organisation is committed to supporting the development of its people
	People are encouraged to improve their own and other people's performance
	People believe their contribution to the organisation is recognised
	The organisation is committed to ensuring equality of opportunity in the development of its people
Planning An Investor in People is clear about its aims and its objectives and what its people need to do to achieve them	The organisation has a plan with clear aims and objectives which are understood by everyone
	The development of people is in line with the organisation's aims and objectives
	People understand how they contribute to achieving the organisation's aims and objectives
Action An Investor in People develops its people effectively in order to improve its performance	Managers are effective in supporting the development of people
	People learn and develop effectively
Evaluation An Investor in People understands the impact of its investment in people on its performance	The development of people improves the performance of the organisation, teams and individuals
	People understand the impact of the development of people on the performance of the organisation, teams and individuals
	The organisation gets better at developing its people

ISO 9000

ISO is the International Organisation for Standardisation. It is made up of national standards institutes from countries across the world. It develops technical standards for all types of organisations and sectors.

ISO 9000, one of the most widely known standards, is an internationally recognised standard for quality management systems. It originates from the British Standard BS 5970. The standard's origins are in the manufacturing sector but it is now used by organisations in all sectors.

The most recent version of the standard, ISO 9000:2000, is based around eight quality management principles:

1 Customer focus

2 Leadership

3 Involvement of people

4 Process approach

5 Systems approach to management

6 Continual improvement

7 Factual approach to decision-making

8 Mutually beneficial suppliers relationships.

Once an organisation has implemented a system that meets the standard it can apply for accreditation. This means that the organisation can advertise the fact that it has an approved quality management system.

It is important to remember that ISO 9000 accreditation is for the quality system and not for the products or services that the organisation provides. Beware of organisations that claim their products are manufactured to ISO 9000 – they are not.

ISO is also responsible for many other standards, some generic, and some specific to sectors, products or services.

ISO 14000 – an environmental management standard – is also becoming more widely used in all sectors.

PROBE

PROBE (Promoting Business Excellence) is a questionnaire-based diagnostic benchmarking tool developed to give organisations a snapshot of their current state. It is managed by the University of Northumbria at Newcastle (UNN) for the CBI and is based on work published in 1998 as an International Service Study by Richard Chase, Aleda Roth and Chris Voss.

PROBE covers the practices and performance across a broad range of issues:

- business leadership
- service processes
- people
- performance management
- results.

Each of these areas is examined in detail to establish the organisation's current practices.

PROBE steps

The PROBE benchmarking process is team-based and consists of the steps outlined below.

Team selection Individuals are chosen from across the organisation and from different management levels. They are people who are able and prepared to contribute to the discussion.

Initial communication The team leader acts as the point of communication to team members. Leaders distribute the team member procedures, guidelines and questionnaires to the team.

Questionnaire The individuals on the team complete the questionnaire before meeting (consulting with colleagues where appropriate).

First meeting The team leader arranges the first team meeting, which lasts a half day (maximum recommended time 3 to 4 hours) to enable discussion and reflection of the individual scores, reaching a team consensus score where possible.

Facilitated day An accredited facilitator leads the facilitated day with the team members, ideally held within 1 to 2 weeks of the first meeting. Summary results from the exercise are presented to the team at the end of this day. A written summary report is submitted by the facilitator, normally within 10 working days. This report will highlight the strengths and weaknesses of the organisation.

Action planning day The facilitator revisits the organisation to work through key issues with the team.

Learning PROBE

The Learning and Skills Development Agency (LSDA) has developed a version of the tool that is designed specifically for the learning and skills sector – Learning PROBE. The tool is readily applicable to colleges and training providers throughout the sector but at the same time ensures full compatibility with the non-education-based version – Service PROBE.

Quality gurus

This chapter summarises the ideas of four well-known quality gurus: Crosby, Deming, Ishikawa and Juran. Their work has been used as a foundation for much quality theory over the past 50 years. There are, however, many other specialists who have contributed to the advancement of quality theory and practice. Some of these are also identified.

Crosby

Philip R Crosby was born in 1926. The Crosby philosophy is that quality is free and that the goal of any system should be zero defects. It is based on 'four absolutes of quality':

- the definition of quality is conformance to requirements
- quality is achieved by prevention rather than inspection
- the quality standard should be zero defects
- the measurement of quality is the price of non-conformance.

Crosby identified a 14-step quality improvement process:

1 establish that management is committed to quality improvement
2 form a quality improvement team
3 establish the actual quality of the process, product or service
4 evaluate the cost of quality (price of non-conformance)
5 raise quality awareness across the entire organisation
6 take corrective actions
7 plan a zero defects programme
8 give all staff training in quality
9 hold a zero defects day
10 ensure that staff and departments set goals for improvement

11 ensure that staff identify causes of errors and
are given management support to remove them

12 recognise all improvements and all staff involved in the improvements

13 establish quality councils

14 do it all over again.

Deming

W Edwards Deming was born in 1900. He is most famous for his
work on quality in Japan. He began teaching in Japan in 1950 at the
request of the Japanese Union of Scientists and Engineers (JUSE);
the Deming Prize for Quality began the following year, 1951.

Deming's philosophy, summarised in his '14 points', is that quality
can only be achieved by adopting an organisation-wide commitment
to continuous improvement and training, and by ensuring that
all people work together, removing barriers between departments
and between staff and management. There is an emphasis
on the psychology of motivation for both staff and managers
in Deming's philosophy.

Deming's 14 points are:

1 create constancy of purpose towards improvement
of product and service

2 adopt the new philosophy

3 cease dependence on mass inspection

4 end the practice of awarding business on the basis of price

5 constantly improve the system of production and service

6 institute training

7 institute leadership

8 drive out fear

9 break down barriers between departments and staff

10 eliminate slogans for staff

11 eliminate numerical goals and management by objective

12 remove barriers that stop staff having pride in their work,
such as annual ratings and merit payments

13 institute a vigorous programme of education and training for all staff

14 take action to accomplish the transformation.

Ishikawa

Kaoru Ishikawa was born in 1915. His theories are based on the belief that quality improvement is a continuous process. He developed a system of seven basic quality tools that can be used to support this continuous improvement. The tools are designed so that staff at all levels can use them without having to undergo excessive training.

Ishikawa's seven basic tools are:

- cause and effect diagrams
- check sheets
- control charts
- flowcharts
- histograms
- Pareto diagrams
- scatter diagrams.

His philosophy promotes the use of quality circles and the involvement of staff at all levels in the quality process. It also stresses the importance of management support to ensure the quality of an organisation's products or services.

Juran

Joseph M Juran was born in 1904. He defined quality as fitness for purpose and stated that the customer's needs should inform process, product and service design. Like Deming, he believed that staff are not the main cause of poor quality, and that less than 20% of problems are caused by an organisation's staff.

His philosophy is based around three specific areas; his 'quality trilogy':

- quality planning
- quality control
- quality improvement.

He identified 10 steps in the quality improvement cycle:

1 build awareness of the need and opportunity for improvement
2 set goals for improvement
3 organise to reach the goals
4 provide training throughout the organisation
5 carry out projects to solve problems
6 report progress
7 give recognition
8 communicate results
9 keep score of any improvements
10 maintain momentum by making improvement part of the processes and systems of the organisation.

Other gurus

Feigenbaum

Arman V Feigenbaum's philosophy promotes the use of organisation-wide systematic quality methods that involve all staff and areas of an organisation.

Moller

Claus Moller asserted that the cornerstone of quality within an organisation is the personal development of its staff. Many of his ideas are based around identifying the ideal performance (IP) and actual performance (AP) levels of staff and how to improve the AP.

Peters

Tom Peters stated that leadership is key to an organisation. His theories promotes the concept of MBWA – management by walking about. They also place great emphasis on the customer focus of an organisation. His more recent work focused on the need for innovation, summarised as 'distinct or extinct', and the need for organisations to make the most of women as customers and employees.

Shingo

Shigeo Shingo is best known for his concept of Poka-Yoke, a method of foolproofing that prevents mistakes being made. His theories emphasise the need to set up systems that will, by their design, always produce quality products or services.

Taguchi

Genichi Taguchi's ideas place the emphasis of quality in the pre-production of products or services. His theory is that quality and reliability are the result of the design of services and products rather than inspection.

Quality jargon buster

BEM Business Excellence Model Now known as the
EFQM Excellence Model

BQF British Quality Foundation The BQF is a not-for-profit
membership organisation promoting business excellence in
all sectors

BSI British Standards Institute Responsible for standards
across a wide range of sectors ; awards the 'Kitemark'

DTI Department of Trade and Industry Government department
that focuses mainly on the needs of business. It produces many
good-practice guides that are applicable to the learning sector

EFQM European Foundation for Quality Management EFQM was
founded in 1988 and has more than 800 members. It was responsible
for developing the EFQM Excellence Model in 1991 (see page 38)

IiP Investors in People Investors in People is an award that
is given to organisations that meet criteria laid down for training
and development of their staff (see page 39)

IQA Institute of Quality Assurance A membership organisation
for the promotion of quality practices

ISO International Organisation for Standardisation ISO develops
technical standards for all types of organisations and sectors. ISO 9000
is its standard for quality management systems (see page 41)

JIT just in time Producing and purchasing products just in time
for delivery to avoid building up large stock levels. It can save
a considerable amount of money but must be well planned
and should incorporate a good quality management system

MBWA management by walking about The theory that managers should manage an organisation by getting to know front-line staff and their work. It ensures that managers have a better understanding of the issues that arise outside the management team

MoT moment of truth The moment when a customer comes into direct contact with a member of staff (see page 31)

PDSA plan, do, study, act A systematic method of improving processes, services or products

PROBE Promoting Business Excellence
A diagnostic benchmarking tool (see page 42)

QA quality assurance A method of assuring the quality of the final goods or services as well as the quality of the processes (see page 4)

QC quality control A method of controlling quality through monitoring and measurement (see page 3)

RQA Raising Quality and Achievement Programme A programme within the Learning and Skills Development Agency that offers support on quality issues

SPC statistical process control Used predominately in a manufacturing context. SPC is a method of controlling the quality of a process by using systematic measurement and monitoring techniques

SWOT strengths, weaknesses, opportunities, threats
SWOT analysis is a useful framework on which to assess a situation (see page 36)

TQM total quality management TQM is a management model that is based on the philosophy that quality is everyone's responsibility. It involves integrating quality systems into every aspect of an organisation's operation (see page 4)

UKAS United Kingdom Accreditation Service UKAS is the sole national body for the accreditation of testing and calibration laboratories, certification and inspection bodies

Next steps

Remember that quality is not just about meeting the standards set down by external agencies or about passing inspections. It is about ensuring that you constantly meet the needs of all of your customers.

If you want to find out more about quality theories and quality tools there are many resources available.

The Raising Quality and Achievement (RQA) Programme within LSDA was established to support the sector in this area. Details of support are listed on the RQA website. There are also downloadable publications available.

Other organisations also offer resources and information. The DTI site, in particular, has downloadable publications on many management theories.

Details of useful websites are given under 'Further information'.

Further information

Books

Dale BG. *Managing quality* (3rd edn). Blackwell Publishers, Malden Massachusetts, 1999.

DTI. *Statistical process control: an introduction to quality improvement*. URN 95/656 DTI Publications, 1995.

DTI. *From quality to excellence*. URN 00/1226 DTI Publications, 2000.

Evans JR, Lindsay WM. *The management and control of quality* (5th edn). West Publishing Company, St Paul, Minnesota, 2001.

Oakland JS. *TQM* (2nd edn). Butterworth-Heinemann, 2000.

Owen J. *College guide to benchmarking*. LSDA, 2000.

Owen J. *Consultancy for free*. LSDA, 2001.

Websites

Charter Mark www.chartermark.gov.uk
This site gives details of Charter Mark criteria and has background information on some organisations that have gone for the award.

DTI (Department of Trade and Industry) www.dti.gov.uk
The site has lots of useful information on quality issues and general management theory. There is also access to a number of useful downloadable publications.

EFQM (European Foundation for Quality Management) www.efqm.org
This site gives background information on the EFQM, details of the Quality Model, and explains how to apply for the award.

IQA (Institute of Quality Assurance) www.iqa.org
The site gives details of the Institute and the services it offers.

LSDA (Learning and Skills Development Agency) www.LSDA.org.uk
The site shows all of the support available from the Agency. There is also access to a considerable number of downloadable publications.

RQA (Raising Quality and Achievement) www.rqa.org.uk
The RQA site lists details of the support available to the sector from the Benchmarking and Information strand and from each of the other strands within the programme.

Example code of conduct for process benchmarking

Preparation

Demonstrate commitment by being prepared before making an initial benchmarking contact.

Make the most of your benchmarking partner's time by being fully prepared for each meeting.

Help your benchmarking partners prepare by providing them with a questionnaire and agenda before benchmarking visits.

Contact

Respect the culture of partner organisations and work within mutually agreed procedures.

Use the preferred contact(s) designated by the partner organisation.

Agree how far communication or responsibility is to be delegated in the course of the benchmarking exercise. Check mutual understanding.

Obtain an individual's permission before providing their name in response to a contact request.

Exchange

Be willing to provide the same type and level of information that you request from your benchmarking partner to your benchmarking partner.

Clarify expectations and avoid misunderstanding by establishing the scope of the project as early as possible.

Be honest.

Confidentiality

Treat benchmarking findings as confidential to the individuals and organisations involved. Such information must not be communicated to third parties without prior consent; make sure that you specify clearly what information is to be shared, and with whom.

An organisation's participation in a study is confidential and should not be communicated externally without their prior permission.

Use of information

Use information obtained through benchmarking only for purposes stated and agreed with the benchmarking partner.

The use or communication of a benchmarking partner's name with the data obtained or the practices observed requires the prior permission of that partner.

Contact lists or other contact information provided by benchmarking networks or databases will only be used for benchmarking.

Legality

If there is any potential question on the legality of an activity, you should take legal advice.

Avoid discussions or actions that could lead to or imply anti-competitive practices. Don't discuss your pricing policy with competitors.

Do not obtain information by any means that could be interpreted as improper.

Do not disclose or use any confidential information that may have been obtained through improper means, or that was disclosed by another in violation of duty of confidentiality.

Do not pass on benchmarking findings to another organisation without first getting the permission of your benchmarking partner and without first ensuring that the data is appropriately anonymous so that the participants' identities are protected.

Completion

Follow through each commitment made to your benchmarking partner in a timely manner.

Try to complete each benchmarking project to the satisfaction of all benchmarking partners.

Understanding and agreement

Understand how your benchmarking partner would like to be treated, and treat them in that way.

Agree how your partner expects you to use the information provided, and do not use it in any way that would break that agreement.